THINKING BIG

THINKING BIG

THE STORY OF A YOUNG DWARF

text and photographs
by Susan Kuklin

Lothrop, Lee & Shepard Books   New York

The author wishes to thank the following for their help in the creation of this book:
Marilyn and Dave Osborn and their children, Jaime and Matthew
Betty Adelson
Katherine Koos
Little People of America
Dr. Charles I. Scott, Jr., at the Alfred I. du Pont Institute
Ann Conlon, teachers, parents, and students at the Alfred Vail School
in Morris Plains, New Jersey
Sharon Steinhoff
Jane Wilson

2 3 4 5 6 7 8 9 10

Library of Congress Cataloging in Publication Data
Kuklin, Susan.   Thinking big.
Summary: Text and photographs depict the life of an eight-year-old dwarf who lives in an average-sized family and attends a regular school.
1. Osborn, Jaime—Juvenile literature. 2. Achondroplasia—Patients—United States—Biography—Juvenile literature. 3. Dwarfs—United States—Biography—Juvenile literature. [1. Achondroplasia. 2. Dwarfs. 3. Physically handicapped.
4. Osborn, Jaime] I. Title. RJ482.A250835 1986   362.1'9892'71 [B]   85-10425
ISBN 0-688-05826-4
ISBN 0-688-05827-2 (lib. bdg.)

To Little People
and
to Bailey, with love

Wherever Jaime Osborn goes, she stands out. When her parents take her places, people stare. Sometimes they come up to her and pat her on the head as if she were a puppy. Strangers ask her questions like, "How old are you?" Jaime says, "I'm eight." Generally, she can guess what's coming next. If they know how big an average eight-year-old is, they might ask, "Are you a midget?"

Jaime doesn't mind explaining why she is so small. "My limbs did not grow as long as other people's," she says, "because I'm a dwarf. Dwarfs are supposed to be small." Most people don't understand that a midget is short all over, while a dwarf like Jaime has short arms and legs on an average-size body.

Jaime's brother, Matthew, is five years old. He is not a dwarf and is much taller than his big sister. Most dwarfs have average-size parents, brothers, and sisters in their families. Matthew says, "I love my sister. She is a very good sister. I like her as a dwarf. It doesn't matter what she is."

Jaime likes it that Matthew is bigger because he can do some favors for her. When she sold Girl Scout Cookies, for example, she took Matthew along. "I'm a good seller," she says. "People can't say no, but first I have to get them to open their doors. That's where Matthew comes in. I can't reach the doorbells. He does it for me."

Jaime also does favors for Matthew. Her brother is only five and cannot read. But Jaime is an excellent reader. Matthew loves having a smart, big sister to play with and to teach him numbers and the ABC's.

To Jaime, it often seems as if the world were built for giants. Every morning, when she and Matthew go downstairs for breakfast, Jaime has to go down the steps differently than other eight-year-olds. Imagine what it would be like to walk up and down stairs that hit you at the knee. That's what it's like for Jaime. Going up means hiking one foot as high as her other knee, shifting her body from one side to the other, and pulling herself up. Coming down is much easier. She sits and slides to the bottom.

When they are downstairs, if their parents aren't up, Matthew and Jaime make their own breakfast. Jaime can reach only as high as the second shelf of the refrigerator. The milk and jelly are higher, so Matthew gets them for her. If Matthew isn't nearby, she just kicks off her shoes and climbs into the refrigerator to get them herself. But she must move fast. Her feet get cold.

Before she goes out, Jaime sits patiently while her mother curls her hair. "I like looking pretty," says Jaime.

On school days, Jaime's mother puts her on the bus. She lifts her up to the top of the steps. At first, when Jaime left the bus, she would sit down and bounce down the steps. The driver complained that this wasn't safe. So now, even though she would prefer getting off the bus by herself, one of her friends holds her hand and helps her.

"Hi, this is your lucky day. You've just met your first dwarf!" Jaime told Lamont when they met. Lamont is the smartest boy in the whole third grade. He's also the tallest. Lamont and Jaime are best buddies.

When Jaime sits at her desk, her feet, unlike the other children's, do not touch the ground. For a long time she let them dangle in midair, but they would fall asleep. That hurt. Then her mother brought a stool to place under the desk. Now Jaime can rest her feet and not worry about them.

Jaime has a special team of friends who sit with her at the number one reading table. When the teacher asks a question, Jaime's hand usually shoots up first. She loves to read out loud or answer the teacher's questions. Jaime is never shy when it comes to speaking out. Even the teacher agrees that Jaime has the loudest voice in the whole class.

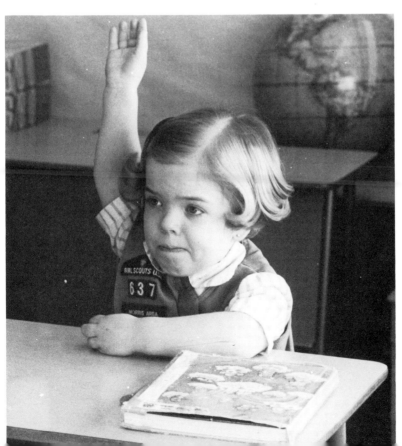

With such short legs holding up her average-size body, it is hard for Jaime to stand or walk for a long time. When she goes on hikes with her class, the other children usually get way ahead. Sometimes, when Jaime runs to catch up, she loses her balance and falls forward. Jaime falls a lot, but she never cries.

Although Jaime wants to be treated just like everyone else, that's not always possible. In gym, she must wear knee pads because her joints are not as strong as other children's. Grandma Mimi made special ones for her. They say "Big J. O." Lamont helps Jaime in gym, especially when they play basketball.

One subject in which Jaime needs no help is art. She is so good that her classmates come to her for help with their drawings. In fact, Jaime says she may become an artist when she grows up. In art, Jaime sits with her team, her best girlfriends from her reading group.

During lunch recess, Jaime likes to ride the small seesaw with her friends. "Sometimes they want to go on the big one," she says, "and I can't play on it. So I go somewhere by myself." Everyone cannot always do small-scale things. Jaime knows that.

"The kindergarteners can be nasty," Jaime recalls. "They may call me names. They say, 'Look at that little baby, look at that little baby.' I tell them that I'm *not* a baby. I'm supposed to be little. I'm a dwarf. If they don't pay attention to what I tell them, I just ignore them. Besides, everybody is a little bit different." Once Jaime's teacher asked her if the children hurt her feelings. She said, "No way…no, ma'am!" Jaime is proud of who she is.

There is one thing that is a terrific struggle for Jaime—her weight. All kinds of problems can occur if dwarfs get fat, since they carry average-size bodies on very short legs. Therefore, she must be careful about how much food she eats.

At birthday parties and after school, Jaime can't have as much chocolate milk or cookies as other children can. Sometimes watching her weight is discouraging. When you're small, a single cookie goes a long way. To lose just three pounds is tough, and frequently the weight seems to come right back.

Jaime told her second-grade teacher, Mrs. Roth, about her weight problem. Mrs. Roth said that she, too, must watch her weight. They agreed to work on it together, and they discuss it each morning.

However, there are some things Jaime can do that most people can't. Dwarfs are double-jointed and can rise from a sitting position on the floor without using

their hands. Jaime can hold a dinner plate on her lap and just pop up. When Matthew tries that, he falls over and spills food from the plate. Matthew is not double-jointed.

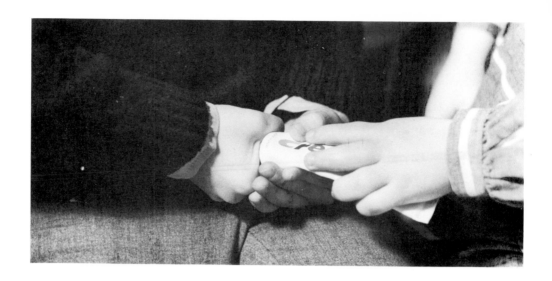

Most dwarfs' fingers are short. This gives Jaime some problems. There is not much strength in Jaime's hands. Getting a tight cap off a toothpaste tube can be difficult, and she appreciates Matthew's help with that.

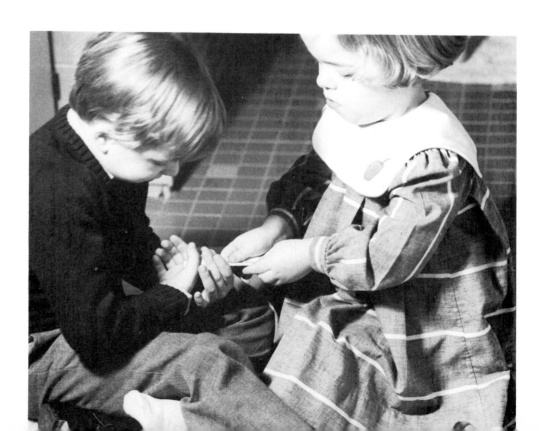

Like most dwarfs, Jaime isn't as bothered by cold temperatures as most average-size people are. Jaime's mom says she is a little hot-water bottle. Everyone in the house but Jaime has an electric blanket. In the summer, however, she would gladly trade, if she could, being a hot-water bottle for being a bowl of ice cubes.

The Osborn family belongs to a group called Little People of America. It is important that Jaime get to know other dwarfs. Jaime likes being around people who are like herself. She and her special friend Corin are always glad to see each other.

Little People of America also helps Jaime's parents understand what is special about being a dwarf. At the meetings they learn from older dwarfs and from doctors just what life will be like for Jaime when she is grown. Little People of America has a motto: Think big. That's Jaime's motto too.

There are lots of outings and parties at Little People meetings and conventions. For Halloween, there were a magician and games with prizes. The manager at the hotel provided a special platform for the video games so the children could reach the controls and see the screens.

At one meeting, Jaime stared into the mirror and said, "Oh, if I stretch back like this, my bottom doesn't stick out so much. But then my stomach sticks out farther." The teenage dwarfs explained to her, "That's the way dwarfs are built. It's the 'dwarf look.'" Jaime admires the dwarf teenagers and likes the way they look.

Jaime loves visiting Suzy Baker. Suzy is seventeen years old and understands what life is like for Jaime, because she is a dwarf and remembers being Jaime's age. She tells Jaime about her own life so Jaime will know what may happen to her in the future.

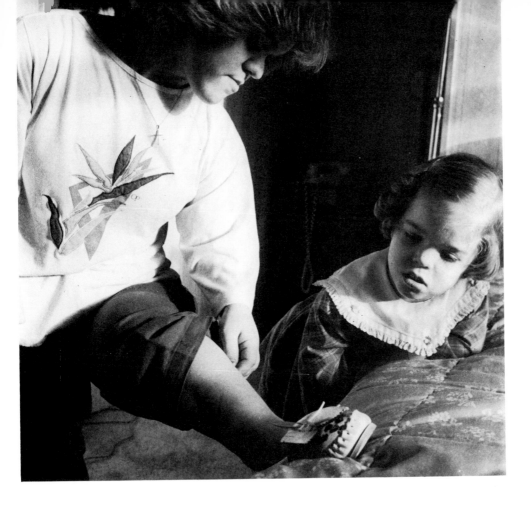

Suzy shows Jaime the tiny scars on her legs from the operation she had recently to make her legs straight. Dwarfs' legs tend to bend outward because their bones can't bear weight the way tall people's can. Jaime will have to wait until she's fully grown to know if she will need the same operation.

Like Suzy, Jaime has clothes specially made for her. Her mom buys regular-size children's clothing and cuts the sleeves and legs down to Jaime's size. Mrs. Osborn says they get free dust rags along with Jaime's clothing.

Once a year, Jaime and her family visit Dr. Scott. Jaime is not sick. Pills or shots won't change the fact that she's a dwarf, just as pills or shots won't change a person's eye color or skin color. That only happens in make-believe stories like *Alice in Wonderland*. Jaime knows you can't always believe what you read about little people in make-believe stories.

Dr. Scott is a specialist. He takes care of many dwarfs. He watches their growing patterns. He measures Jaime's head, back, arms, and legs with a tape measure. Then he checks all her joints. At her latest checkup, Jaime was worried because she had promised the doctor she would lose four pounds, and she had lost only one and a half. When Dr. Scott checked her weight, he said, "Look, Jaime, don't worry. Even though you didn't lose that much weight, you are two centimeters taller. The extra weight was changed to height. You did a fine job. In fact, you get an *A*."

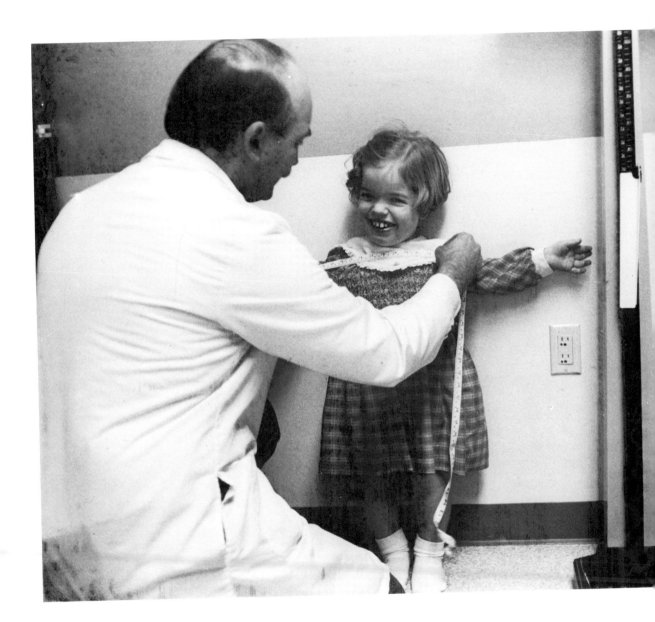

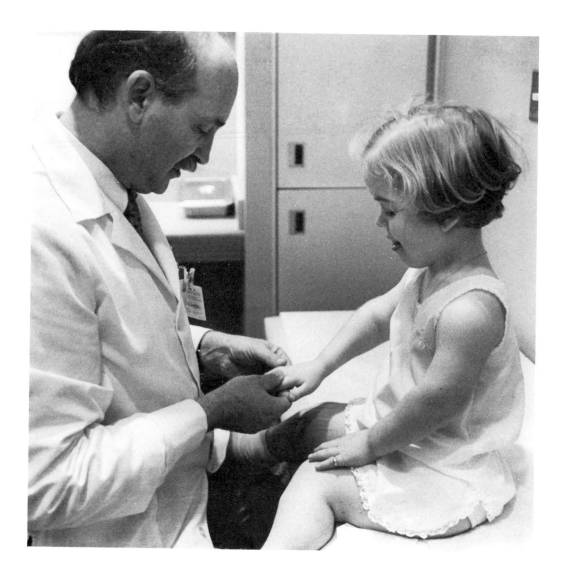

"Now put your fingers together, Jaime," he said. "If you're a *real* Little Person, you can't make all your fingers touch." "You bet I'm a real Little Person," said Jaime. "*Look*." And she showed her tightly squeezed fingers, grouped two and two.

As they leave Dr. Scott's office, Jaime's dad saw that she was getting very tired. He scooped her up in his arms and carried her. Jaime laughed and said, "Oh boy, I'm glad I have a big, strong dad who can carry me."

Once Jaime's mom asked her, "Do you know what Mommy and Daddy think about sometimes? We wonder if you have ever wished that we were dwarfs." Jaime thought about it for a moment and said, "I wish you were dwarfs 'cause then you'd be like me and our house would be the size of all of us. That way I could help you more. You wouldn't have to trip over my stools and stuff." Jaime's mother put her arms around her and said, "Mommy and Daddy never mind your stools at all. In fact, we bless them."

Jaime's parents always try to be honest with her in a gentle way. They don't want to make believe she will be taller when she won't. They want her to understand that though she is a dwarf, if she thinks big, she can do many big things. That goes for everyone. Jaime knows that's true. Outside she is small, but inside she is big. As she says, "I am like everybody else, just little."

EPILOGUE

There are many different types of dwarfism. Jaime Osborn is an achondroplastic dwarf, the most common variety. This condition is caused by a genetic abnormality affecting primarily the skeletal system. It neither limits her life span nor affects her intellectual capabilities.

The probability of two average-size parents producing a child with Jaime's kind of dwarfism is one in forty thousand. A chance event, or mutation, occurs in one of the parents and results in a gene that causes achondroplasia. When this will happen cannot be predicted, and the source of the mutated gene cannot be determined afterward.

The chance of the Osborns having a second dwarf child is again one in forty thousand. Indeed, their son, Matthew, is even tall for his age.

When Jaime has a child of her own, the chance of its being a dwarf will depend upon her husband. If he is average-size, then there is a fifty–fifty chance that each child they have will be average-size. If her husband is an achondroplastic dwarf, then there is a twenty-five-percent chance that the offspring will be average-size. Each average-size child born to either one or two dwarf parents has the same one-in-forty-thousand chance of having a dwarf child. The average-size child does not carry the syndrome.

Not long after she was born, the doctors recognized in Jaime a number of physical characteristics that identify an achondroplast. For the first three months of Jaime's life, Marilyn and Dave Osborn did not know that she was a dwarf. When they learned about it, the next few months were difficult for them. Marilyn refused to leave her daughter until she was asleep for the night and weaning Jaime was hard for her. She recalls feeling, for the first time in her life, that there was something wrong she couldn't fix. The Osborns moved from their home in St. Louis back to Texas, where both their families lived. Having grandparents close by when Jaime was young was healing for Marilyn and Dave. The family regrouped, and together they learned about dwarfism, mainly through Little People of America. Another organization that can help families in situations like this is the Human Growth Foundation.

At the age of five and a half, Jaime began having difficulty breathing. She had little manual strength, and her balance seemed off. Dr. Charles I. Scott, a leading pediatric geneticist who specializes in dwarfism, examined her. He found that the opening at the base of her skull was not wide enough and was squeezing her spinal cord. This interfered with the neurological reflexes that flow back and forth between the nerve endings and the brain. She needed an operation to widen the hole. If she did not have the surgery, she would suffocate within the year.

The operation took four hours. After the surgery her breathing remained abnormal, and she was on a ventilator in the intensive care unit for eight days. This gave the family many anxious moments. There was a great risk that Jaime would contract pneumonia. However, she regained her strength quickly and left the hospital in two weeks. She entered first grade a month later.

As a dwarf, Jaime is susceptible to physiological problems relating to her bone and nervous systems. When she reaches adolescence, she may need orthopedic surgery to correct the bowing in her legs. Dr. Scott monitors her yearly.

Even though Jaime has many dwarf friends through her association with Little People of America, she is the only dwarf person at her school. Jaime has always been popular with her average-size classmates. However, when they reach adolescence there will be boy–girl pairing off, and it is probable that Jaime will not be as close to her classmates as she is now. Many dwarfs develop other interests in their early teen years to fill the void they feel from being ignored. The most difficult time is usually from the ages of twelve to about sixteen. In the later teens, dwarfs tend to once again participate in the social life of their average-size friends.

The Osborns are well aware of this possible future problem and know that Jaime will be hurt if she is left out. Marilyn says, "It is a blessing to have older LPA's who can guide us through that. With tremendous support from friends, family, skillful doctors, and many, many prayers, we got through her surgery. She's doing so well now. We see her becoming more and more independent every day. We'll take care of future problems as they arise. I'm so thankful that we're alive and well and together today. That's all that one can ask. If we can make the quality of the time we have now the very highest, then that will be the best preparation for any difficulties she may face in the future."

Jaime is a friendly, self-assured child. She has an extraordinary sense of compassion and frequently expresses concern for the unfortunate. She talks of becoming an artist or a librarian (she loves books) or a teacher. Jaime says, "Maybe I should teach kindergarten. Then I'd be helping kids even littler than me."